MIND MATTERS

A BOOK ON MENTAL STATUS EXAMINATION

AF528467

Indira

BlueRose ONE
Stories Matter

© Indira 2022

All rights reserved

All rights reserved by author. No part of this publication may be reproduced, stored in a retrieval system or transmitted in any form or by any means, electronic, mechanical, photocopying, recording or otherwise, without the prior permission of the author.

Although every precaution has been taken to verify the accuracy of the information contained herein, the author and publisher assume no responsibility for any errors or omissions. No liability is assumed for damages that may result from the use of information contained within.

First Published in December 2022

ISBN: 978-93-5704-457-8

BLUEROSE PUBLISHERS

www.BlueRoseONE.com

info@bluerosepublishers.com

+91 8882 898 898

Cover Design:

Aman Sharma

Typographic Design:

Namrata Saini

Distributed by: BlueRose, Amazon, Flipkart

This book is dedicated to
my ever-curious and enthusiastic students
who keep the quest for knowledge alive in me.

Preface

"Don't just learn, experience. Don't just read, absorb. Don't just think, ponder." — Roy T. Bennett.

Dear Readers

Necessity is the mother of invention.

This proverb may sound cliché, but this book is definitely inspired by the blank looks I received from my students in my class on Psychiatric Symptomatology.

After completing the whole chapter of Mental Status Examination, not only undergraduates, even the postgraduate students will invariably discuss 'hallucination' under the heading of 'thought' and write 'delusion' as a 'perceptual disorder'.

This book is nothing but a compilation of the classroom notes I empower my students with based on an extensive review of available literature. All explanations are based on student-teacher interaction in the class, all examples are derived from the experience they can relate to.

As I always tell in my class, if you learn to conduct the Mental Status Examination in general, no disease condition pertaining to mental health will be difficult to appreciate.

I sincerely wish this book enhances the joy of learning, consolidate your comprehension and enable you to translate the theory into clinical practice.

Jai Hind!

Author

Foreword

It is an honour to present this book 'Mind matters' to the readers. A complex topic like psychiatric symptomatology is immaculately dealt by the author. Mental status examination is an indispensible part of assessment in the field of Psychiatry and Psychology. The author explained each part with minute details which reflects years of experience and expertise in the topic. The format attached for conducting MSE is an added point which makes the procedure very comprehensive for the beginners. Even the PG students and practicing mental health professionals will be thoroughly benefitted with the explanations given in this book.

This is the first book by the author but reading this I got acquainted with the exclusive caliber she possesses. Apart from the content adequacy and validity, the organization of the material captures the literary skill of the author and intrigues the reader to continue reading. It is a handy book one can carry anywhere.

My compliments to the author for contributing this piece of brilliance to the literature of Psychology and looking forward for more of such creativity. I am sure the readers will also have similar cognizance once they go through this book.

Dr B Vengamma
DM Neurology
Director cum Vice Chancellor
SVIMS

Index

CHAPTER 1

Introduction to MSE

"Biology gives you a brain. Life turns it into a mind."
- Jeffrey Kent Eugenides

Brain is the most vital organ living beings are blessed with. The average adult male brain weighs 1336 grams, which is 138 grams heavier than the female counterpart. Apart from the 60% of fat as major constituent, the brain comprises more than 100 billion neurons, trillions of synapses with a complex network of electric impulses, channels, action potentials and vasculature. The various functions involve cognitive abilities, control of emotions, fine-tuning of sensations, perceptions and motor activities, regulation of autonomic functions such as breathing, temperature, respiration, heart rate, sleep-wake cycles, coughing, sneezing, digestion, vomiting and swallowing.

Brain is totally tangible - one can see a brain through imaging, touch during a surgery, and store in formaldehyde solution in a lab after death.

Mind on the other hand is purely hypothetical, intangible and abstract. The human mind is the most fascinating and complicated concept. Mind is believed to be dealing with emotion, perception, memory, judgment, attention, concentration, creative and critical thinking.

Definition

Mental Status Examination (MSE) is a structured clinical assessment tool to identify and monitor any deviation in mental and behavioral domains from a cross-sectional view which aids in diagnosing a mental health condition and determining the severity.

It is like physical examination in Psychiatry.

Origin

In the Treatise on Insanity, published in 1801, Dr Philippe Pinel, the father of scientific psychiatry, scripted 'To seize the true character of mental derangement in a given case, and to pronounce an infallible prognosis of the event, is often a task of particular delicacy, and requires the united exertion of great discernment, of extensive knowledge and of incorruptible integrity.' This can be considered a conception of modern days' MSE.

In 1918, Adolf Meyer developed a standardized outline to evaluate a patient's mental status in clinical setting. However, some attributes it to German-Swiss Psychiatrist Karl Theodor Jaspers.

Principles involved

1. Empathy

The ability to share another person's feelings and emotions as if they were one's own is called empathy. While conducting an MSE, the interviewer should reflect empathy towards the person being assessed.

2. Trust

Faith on the intention and capacity of another is trust. The interviewer must generate an atmosphere of mutual trust between him and the individual undergoing MSE to extract maximum cooperation.

3. Dignity

The quality of being worthy of respect is termed as dignity. The patient deserves to be treated with dignity, privacy and confidentiality at all point of time.

4. Observation

The action or process of closely monitoring something or someone is termed as observation. The examiner should not rely exclusively on the verbal communication, and must give weightage to the observation as it is a very effective assessment tool.

5. Validity

Here validity means the quality of being logically or factually sound. The inputs given by patient should be tallied with the family, friends and other informants to ascertain authenticity.

Components

1. Appearance and Behaviour
2. Thought and Speech
3. Mood and Affect
4. Perception
5. Cognitive functions

In subsequent chapters, the components will be elaborated upon.

The MSE must be documented with date and time as the patient's responses are likely to change during course of illness and under the influence of treatment.

CHAPTER 2

Appearance & Behaviour

"We do not see people as they are, but as they appear to us". – Robert Greene.

Appearance is the description of how a patient looks during the interview, whereas behaviour is the description obtained by observing how a patient acts at that time. The important point to keep in mind while assessing appearance and behaviour is the educational qualification and socio-cultural background of the patient. The first component of MSE can be described under following heads –

A. General appearance

1. Body built

German psychiatrist Ernst Kretschmer developed a classification system for personality based on four types of body built. According to this asthenic (thin, small, weak) people are more prone to develop Schizophrenia, athletic (muscular, broad-framed) people may develop substance use disorder and pyknic (stocky, fat) have tendency to suffer from Manic Depressive Psychoses. The fourth type, dysplastic (disproportionate body) was not adequately explored. On today's date, it is not necessary to draw an inference based on body built. However it may have a connection with psychological profile of the patient.

Document – Asthenic/ Athletic/ Pyknic/ Dysplastic

2. Age appropriateness

It means if the patient looks his or her stated age.

Document – Age appropriate or Looks older/younger than stated age.

Clinical significance - Looking younger than reported age might signify a developmental delay. Looking older may reflect severe physiological or mental disorders, chronic substance use, grief or stress.

3. Grooming

The level of hygiene and grooming gives an idea of a patient's level of functioning.

Document - Immaculate/ Kempt/ Unkempt

Clinical significance - Poor grooming or hygiene suggests severe Depression, neurocognitive disorder, or negative symptoms of Schizophrenia.

4. Clothing

The dress patient is wearing should be appropriate to weather and occasion.

Document – Clothed as per norm/ Subdued/ Riotous

Clinical significance – Shabby dressing may indicate Depression, whereas gaudy dressing in garish colours with or without exhibitionism (revealing outfits) is indicative of Mania.

5. Accessories

The accessories like multiple piercing, hair colour and tattoos also speak volume about the personality and mood state of the patient.

B. Attitude towards examiner

1. Gestures

Document – Cooperative/ Relaxed/ Agitated/ Avoidant/ Indifferent/ Guarded/ Evasive/ Hostile/ Combative/ Haughty/ Playful/ Over-friendly/ Hallucinatory (smiling or crying without apparent reason)/ muttering or talking to self/ odd gesturing/ Compulsive (performing a repetitive action).

Clinical significance – Agitated and avoidant may suggest Depression, whereas indifferent, guarded, hallucinatory and evasive is more likely to be Schizophrenia. Hostile, combative, haughty and over-friendly is suggestive of Mania, compulsive suggests Obsessive Compulsive Disorder (OCD).

2. Facial expression

Document – Smiling/ Grimacing (facial contortion)/ Perplexed (puzzled bewilderment)/ Apathetic/ Frowning/ Tearful/ Silly smile.

Clinical significance – Grimacing may suggest organic pathology. Perplexity, apathy can be suggestive of Schizophrenia, frowning and tearfulness in Depression and silly smile can be in post Epilepsy and Schizophrenia.

The omega sign (two vertical slits between the eye-brows, joined at the top by a horizontal crease) is considered associated with severe Depression. Also, Veraguth folds (diagonal palpebral folds running medially upward) is believed to be a sign of chronic Depression.

3. Eye contact

It is a very informative part of non-verbal communication. Direct eye contact conveys honesty, interest and attentiveness in a communication.

Document – Direct/ Furtive (hidden glance)/ Nil; Continuous/ Intermittent

Clinical significance – Schizophrenics have a tendency to avoid eye contact, patients with Anxiety maintains it, whereas Manic patients may do an excessive scanning.

4. Social etiquettes

Document – Appropriate/ Inappropriate

Clinical significance – Inappropriate social etiquettes suggest Psychoses or Mania.

5. Rapport

Development of an empathetic and working relationship between examiner and patient is called rapport.

Document – Rapport built with ease/ Built with difficulty/ Not built at all.

Clinical significance – Inability to build a rapport depicts personality issues, social withdrawal or psychotic features which need further exploration.

C. Gait

Gait is the pattern and style of walking. Gait is changed when there is an organic cause. However, patient may have functional gait disorders associated with psychological upheaval.

Document - Dragging of one leg/ Sudden knee buckling or collapse/ Small and slow steps/ Excessive swaying/ Extra movements of arms and legs that disrupt balance/ Crouching/ Anxiety about falling.

Clinical significance – Suggests a neurological condition such as Epilepsy, Migraines, Somatoform disorders, physical or sexual abuse. If the gait is stiff, shuffling or ataxic, may point to Parkinson's disease.

D. Posture

The position in which someone holds his body when standing or sitting is referred to as posture.

Disorders of Posture

i) Negativism – An apparently motiveless resistance showed by the patient to all passive movements or commands by the examiner or doing exactly opposite.

ii) Automatic obedience – Pathological compliance to the tactile or visual stimuli overriding the verbal command.

Example – Patient is instructed not to shake hands with the interviewer, but whenever the interviewer extends his right arm, patient invariably gives a handshake.

iii) Cerea Flexibilitas/ Waxy flexibility – Plastic resistance to passive movements and assumption of odd, uncomfortable position, part of the body appears as flexible as wax.

iv) Catalepsy – Prolonged sustaining of odd posture. Waxy flexibility is the process and catalepsy is the end result.

Example – Patient assumes the position of sitting on an imaginary chair or resting his head on a psychological pillow.

v) Mitmachen – Despite verbal instruction to the contrary, no resistance is shown when light pressure is applied by the examiner to a body part of patient and returns to normal when released.

Example – Patient is instructed not to allow his hand to be lifted by examiner. Even then the patient does not resist while being lifted and lowers immediately as the examiner releases the hold.

vi) Cogwheel rigidity - A cog is a wheel with square or triangular teeth around the edge, which is used in a machine to turn another wheel or part. When a muscle responds with cogwheel-like jerks to the use of constant force in bending the limb, is termed as cogwheel rigidity.

Example – When the examiner applies pressure to extend the hand of the patient, it gives way in little, repeated jerks.

Clinical significance - Negativism, Automatic obedience, Waxy flexibility, Catalepsy and Mitmachen are suggestive of Schizophrenia. Whereas cogwheel rigidity is typical of Parkinsonism, and Extra Pyramidal Symptoms(EPS) as an adverse effect of anti-psychotic treatments.

E. Psychomotor activity (PMA)

"Psychomotor" refers to the connection between mental processes and physical movements.

Quantitative disorders of PMA

PMA can be increased or decreased in certain conditions.

i) Hyperactivity – Increased PMA with or without goal-directed behavior.

Clinical significance - Suggests use of stimulant, Hyperkinetic disorder, Schizophrenia and Mania.

ii) Excitement – Hyperactivity accompanied by emotional arousal.

Clinical significance – Can be present in Schizophrenia and Mania.

iii) Impulsivity – Acting without a fore-thought.

Clinical significance – Can be present in Hyperkinetic disorder and Mania.

iv) Akathisia – A subjective urge to move or inability to stay still.

Clinical significance – Suggestive of Hyperkinetic disorder and adverse effects of antipsychotic drugs.

v) Agitation – Presence of anxiety along with restlessness.

Example – Pacing, fidgeting, foot or finger tapping, talking faster than normal or switching television channels repeatedly

Clinical significance – Typical of Anxiety and Depression.

vi) Psychomotor Retardation/ Bradykinesia - Decreased level of PMA.

Example - Talking slowly, difficulty writing or typing, having trouble getting out of bed, taking a long time in between bites of food, moving slowly, often hunched over with head lowered.

Clinical significance – Suggestive of Catatonic stupor, Depression.

vii) Akinesia – Absence of PMA.

Clinical significance – Suggests Schizophrenia, Severe Depression and Parkinson's.

Qualitative disorders of PMA

i) Tics – Sudden, repetitive, involuntary, non-rhythmic motor movement or vocalization involving discrete muscle groups.

Example – Motor – twitching of face and other body parts. - Vocal - grunting, sniffing, or throat clearing.

Clinical significance – Indicates Gilles de Tourette's Syndrome (GTS).

ii) Mannerisms – Idiosyncratic, personalized movements or activities with or without goal.

Example – Scratching head, pulling one's own nose.

Clinical significance – May not have psychopathology but bizarre ones may suggest Schizophrenia.

iii) Stereotype – Odd, repetitive, uniformed, non-goal directed activity.

iv) Perseveration – repetitive activity tends to persist beyond the point of relevance.

Example – The patient wipes his sweaty face clean with a tissue, and continues to repeat the action several times thereafter.

v) Echopraxia - Automatic mimicking of examiner's action.

Clinical significance – Stereotype, Perseveration, Echopraxia all three are suggestive of Schizophrenia.

Points to ponder

- Appearance and behaviour is assessed under five major heads – general appearance, attitude towards examiner, gait, posture and psychomotor activities.
- General appearance is further described in five subheads – body-built, age appropriateness, grooming, clothing and accessories.
- Attitude towards examiner is further classified explained in five subheads – gestures, facial expressions, eye contact, social etiquettes and rapport.
- Disorders of postures are – negativism, automatic obedience, waxy flexibility, catalepsy, mitmachen and cogwheel rigidity.
- Quantitative changes in PMA are – hyperactivity, akathisia, excitement, agitation, impulsivity, bradykinesia and akinesia.
- Quantitative changes in PMA are – tics, mannerisms, stereotype, perseveration and echopraxia.

CHAPTER 3

Thought and Speech

"In most cases the mouth speaks what the heart is full of." – Jim Beggs

Thinking is a goal-directed flow of ideas, symbols and associations initiated by a problem, characterized by rational connections between successive ideas or thoughts, and lead to a logical conclusion. Therefore, thought process which is not goal-directed, or disjointed, or does not lead to a realistic solution pertaining to the given problem, is considered abnormal.

In MSE, thought can be evaluated under the following heads –

A. Form

The capacity of conceptualization or abstraction is considered the form or structure of thought. Scientists always took interest in formal thought disorders and many of them came up with different classifications, like Cameron, Goldstein and Eugene Bleuler. But the commonly accepted one is by Schneider, in which he described five types -

i) Derailment – Thought slides on to a subsidiary thought.

ii) Substitution – A major thought is replaced by a subsidiary thought.

iii) Omission – Senseless omission of a thought or part of it.

iv) Fusion – Heterogeneous elements of thought are interwoven with each other.

v) Drivelling – Disordered intermixture of constituents parts of a complex thought.

Later, one more type was included –

vi) Desultory thinking – Grammatically and syntactically correct speech but sudden ideas force their way in from time to time.

vii) Associative loosening - Can be another inclusion in formal thought disorders, in which the patient shifts ideas to one another with no logical connections.

Speech – Incoherent (makes no sense to the examiner).

Clinical significance – Suggestive of Schizophrenia and coarse brain disease.

B. Progression

This is a description of the organization of the thoughts expressed by a patient. If form is the anatomy of thought, then progression can be compared to physiology.

Disorders of tempo

i) Flight of ideas – Rapid succession of thoughts, no general direction, any connection appears due to chance factors, easily diverted by external stimuli, but coherent.

Speech - Verbal associations of all kinds, like – assonance, alliteration, clang associations, proverbs and clichés can be incorporated in speech.

Example – Patient's verbatim 'Vikram Singh is our physical trainer, Vikram Singh has no ethics, man must always have ethics in life, life is nothing but a journey….' and so on.

Clinical significance – Typical of Mania, occasionally seen in Schizophrenic excitements and organic disorders with hypothalamic lesions.

ii) Prolixity - Speed of thought is not as fast as flight of ideas, despite many irrelevancies, patient is able to return at the task at hand.

Speech – Pressured.

Clinical significance – Suggestive of Hypomania.

iii) Retardation – The train of thought is slowed down.

Speech – Impoverished.

Clinical significance – Seen in Depression and rare condition of Manic stupor.

Disorders of Continuity

i) Blocking – Sudden arrest of the train of thought, leaving a 'blank'. An entirely new thought may then begin.

Speech – Multiple pauses and delays in response to questions.

Clinical significance – Suggestive of Schizophrenia.

ii) Perseveration - Mental operations tend to persist beyond the point of relevance and thus prevent progress of thinking.

Example – The examiner asks 'Whats your name?' Patient replies 'Jagdish'. Examiner asks another question like 'Whats your father's name?'; Patient sticks to 'Jagdish'. Again, examiner asks 'Which place you belong to?'; Patient's response is 'Jagdish'.

Clinical significance – Common in generalized and localized brain disorders.

Disorders of direction

i) Circumstantiality – Slow but connected thoughts with unnecessary trivial details but finally the goal is reached.

Clinical significance – Outstanding feature of Epileptic personality change.

ii) Tangentiality - A series of connected thoughts that touches the topic like a tangent but do not return to the original topic.

Clinical significance – May be found in Mania, Schizophrenia and Organic disorder.

C. Content

This is essentially the subject matter of the thoughts that are in the patient's mind. It is determined by listening throughout the interview and through direct questioning.

i) Overvalued ideas – A thought which because of the associated feeling, takes precedence over all other ideas and maintains for a significant period of time.

Clinical significance – Present in non-psychotic people with intact personality. However overvalued ideas of jealousy can be a cause of criminal offence.

ii) Fantasies – Vivid imagination with a wishful content perceived as unreal by the individual.

iii) Obsessions – Recurrent, irrational, intrusive, ego-dystonic, ego-alien ideas.

Clinical significance – Suggests OCD, Depression, Schizophrenia and occasionally in organic states like post-encephalitis.

iv) Phobias – Irrational fear.

v) Ideas of reference – False-interpretation with a self-referential tendency. Individual tends to relate random things to own self.

vi) Delusion – A false, unshakable belief, held on inadequate grounds and not compatible with socio-cultural background of the individual.

A belief related to existence of God does not require any ground of evidence as it is supported by the socio-cultural background, hence can not be termed as delusion. But a belief of possessing divine or magical power will qualify for delusion unless proved otherwise.

Classification of Delusion based on Origin

a. Primary/True delusion – There is no preceding morbid psychological phenomenon.

According to Schneider, Primary delusions can be further divided in –

- Delusional mood – The person thinks that something is going on around which concerns him, but does not know what the matter is.
- Delusional/ Apophanous perception – attribution of a new meaning in self-reference to a normally perceived object.
- Sudden delusional idea/ Autochthonous delusion – sudden onset fully-formed delusion.

Clinical significance - Diagnostics of Acute Schizophrenia, occasionally organic states.

b. Secondary/ Delusion like idea – Follows a morbid psychological phenomenon. This kind of delusion is more systematized as it involves several interrelated beliefs logically woven into each other.

Clinical significance – Present in Chronic Schizophrenia and all other types of Psychoses.

Classification of Delusion based on Theme

a. Persecutory delusion - Most common form of delusion in which the person believes he is being stalked, spied upon, obstructed, poisoned, conspired against or harassed by other individuals or an organization.

Clinical significance – Suggestive of Schizophrenia.

b. Delusion of jealousy - Morbid jealousy and delusions of marital infidelity. The condition can be appreciated in William Shakespeare's revolutionary play 'Othello' in which the protagonist who is a military commander, kills his beloved wife in a blind rage because of delusion of infidelity.

Clinical significance – Common in Alcohol addiction, suggestive of coarse brain disease and Schizophrenia.

c. Delusion of love / Erotomania - The patient is usually a young woman who is often firmly convinced that a person she considers to be of higher social and/or professional standing is in love with her. In reality the victim has never encouraged the patient. This feature was first described by G.G. De Clerambault in 1885 and therefore also referred to as De Clerambault's Syndrome.

Clinical significance – Suggestive of Schizophrenia.

d. Delusion of grandeur - The person believes they have an exceptional talent, extravagant wealth or special power.

Clinical significance – Suggestive of Schizophrenia and Mania.

e. Delusion of ill health / Somatic delusion- A person is convinced something is wrong in his body despite negative investigation reports, multiple consultations with physicians and even surgical procedures. In

Hypochondriacal patients, delusion may extend to specific belief that the person is suffering from some incurable disease.

Clinical significance – Most common in Depression, may be present in Schizophrenia and personality disorders.

f. Delusion of guilt – The person believes he is an unpardonable sinner and he ruined his family.

Clinical significance – Typical of Severe Depression.

g. Nihilistic Delusion - The person denies the existence of his body, mind, life, loved ones and world around him.

Clinical significance – Typical of Severe Agitated Depression, occasionally seen in Schizophrenia and Delirium.

h. Delusion of poverty – The person is convinced that he is impoverished and he and his family is facing destitution.

Clinical significance – Typical of Severe Depression.

D. Control/Possession

i) Thought alienation – Patient has an experience that his thoughts are under control of an outside agency. It can be further classified into -

a. Thought Insertion – Foreign thoughts are inserted in his mind by an outside agency.

b. Thought Withdrawal – Thoughts are withdrawn and suddenly disappears from his mind by outside influence which leads to subjective feeling of thought blocking and omission.

c. Thought Diffusion / Broadcasting – Individual thinks his thoughts are escaping the confines of his mind and everyone is thinking in unison with him.

Clinical significance – Typical of Schizophrenia.

E. Speech

Speech is the mirror of thought. Patient's speech allows the interviewer to note the quality of thought process including its flow, logic and associations. Speech is evaluated passively throughout the interview, also can be analyzed through direct questions.

In MSE, speech can be assessed under the following heads -

1. Quantity

Rate, quantity or productivity of speech is an important diagnostic criterion. Different functional conditions which reflect an abnormal speech quantity are –

i) Mutism – Complete absence of speech.

Clinical significance – May be seen in Somatoform disorder, Depression, Catatonic stupor and coarse brain disease, selective mutism (mute in the presence of particular person or situation) present in children.

Differential diagnosis – Aphasia (difficulty with written and spoken language) which has an organic origin.

ii) Poverty of speech - Patient speaks quite less than normal, considered a slow rate.

Clinical significance – Suggestive of Depression, Anxiety and neurocognitive disorders.

iii) Pressure of speech – Patients speaks excessively, referred as high rate of production.

Clinical significance - May indicate acute substance intoxication or Manic episode or some level of Anxiety.

2. Spontaneity and Reaction time

Normally people are spontaneous which means they can initiate a speech. Reaction time is the average length of pause a person takes before responding to another.

Document – Spontaneity present or not; Reaction time normal, delayed or instant.

Clinical significance - A delayed response time may indicate Depression neurocognitive disorder, or thought blocking in Psychoses.

3. Rhythm and Flow

Any hesitancy in continuing the speech can be abnormal.

i) Stammering/ Stuttering/ Cluttering – Normal flow of speech is interrupted by pauses, repetition or fragmentation of words.

Clinical significance – May be present in Anxiety or onset of Schizophrenia.

Differential diagnosis – Dysprosody (a rarest neurological speech disorder characterized by alterations in intensity, the timing of utterance of segments, rhythm, cadency and intonation of words).

ii) Slurring – Indistinct speech.

Clinical significance - May indicate intoxication.

iii) Dysarthria – Difficulty in articulation.

Clinical significance - May indicate a possible motor dysfunction.

4. Volume

Clinical significance - Volume can be low if a patient is depressed or withdrawn. Loud volume suggests Mania, neurocognitive disorder or hearing difficulties.

5. Tone

Tone or intonation is the rise and fall of voice reflecting the emotion while talking.

Clinical significance – Monotonous speech is typical of Schizophrenia. A child-like tone may suggest a developmental delay.

6. Language and Vocabulary

Use of language, vocabulary, diction and accent is supposed to be compatible with the educational qualification and socio-cultural background of people. The speech should have intact syntax (form) and semantics (meaning).

Clinical significance – A child-like syntax may be suggestive of Hebephrenic Schizophrenia.

7. Deviations

i) Neologism – Idiosyncratically coining new words or using existing words in a new context.

Example – Attaching 'vessel' to every object nomenclature, thus clock is 'time vessel' and lamp becomes 'light vessel'.

ii) Echolalia – Repetition, echoing or mimicking of words, phrases or sounds heard by patient in the background.

Example – When examiner asks 'What's your name?', instead of telling own name, patient mimics examiner by asking 'What's your name?'

iii) Cataphasia / Verbigeration – Morbid repetitions of words, phrases or sentences without any provocation.

Example – Patient may continuously repeat phrases like 'Kusum's blue book.. Kusum's blue book.. Kusum's blue book..'

Clinical significance – Neologism, Echolalia and Verbigeration all three are suggestive of Schizophrenia.

iv) Coprolalia – Vocal tics characterized by shouting of obscene words.

Clinical significance – Suggestive of GTS.

Points to ponder

- In MSE, Thought is assessed under four major heads – form, progression, content and possession.
- Formal thought disorders include – derailment, substitution, omission, fusion, driveling, desultory thinking and associative loosening.
- Progression is further assessed under three subheads – tempo or speed, continuity and direction
- Disorders of tempo include flight of ideas, prolixity and thought retardation.
- Disorders of continuity include thought blocking and perseveration.
- Disorders of direction include circumstantiality and tangentiality.
- Disorders of content include overvalued ideas, phobias, obsessions, fantasies, referential ideas and delusions.
- Delusions are further classified based on origin and theme.
- Based on origin, delusions can be primary or secondary.

- Primary delusions are further divided into delusional mood, delusional perception and sudden delusional ideas.
- Based on theme, delusions can be of several types, for example – delusion of persecution, jealousy, love, guilt, poverty, somatic delusion and nihilistic delusion.
- Disorders of possession include thought alienation which is sub-divided into insertion, withdrawal and broadcasting.
- Speech can be assessed through quantity, spontaneity, reaction time, rhythm, flow, volume, tone, language, vocabulary and deviations.
- Disorders of quantity of speech involve mutism, impoverished and pressured speech.
- Disorders of flow involve stammering, slurring and dysarthria.
- Other deviations in speech are neologism, echolalia, verbigeration and coprolalia.

CHAPTER 4

Mood and Affect

"Mood has to be controlled. Otherwise, it's your master."

— Toba Beta

"Mood" is an over-used word in man's vocabulary. However in clinical setting, it is not as volatile as being in mood or not being in mood for a movie or an ice-cream. To understand 'mood', one must start with 'feeling' and 'emotion'.

A feeling can be defined as a positive or negative reaction to single experience. For example – an employee is disappointed because she did not get the recognition she thought she deserved.

Emotion is a short-lived stirred-up state due to physiological changes which occurs as a response to some event which is comparable to fight or flight response described by Hans Selye. A few examples of emotions are – anger, rage, joy, horror and grief.

A. Mood

Mood is a persistent, pervasive, emotional state. Persistent since it sustains for at least weeks and pervasive because it colours the entire experience of the beholder. It is the patient's subjective description of how he is feeling in his own words which is obtained by directly asking him.

In MSE, Mood is assessed under the following heads -

1. Quality

Question – How do you feel?

Document - Patient's response verbatim like 'okay'/ 'happy'/ 'sad'/ 'worried'/ 'irritable'/ 'angry'/ 'detached'/ 'indifferent'.

Clinical significance – An 'okay' suggests euthymic, happy can be suggestive of Hypomania or Mania, similarly a sad or irritable mood may be Depression. If worried signifies Anxiety, angry, detached and indifferent indicates Schizophrenia.

2. Intensity

Question – Can you specify how strong is this feeling?

Document – 'Mild'/ 'very'/ 'extremely'.

Clinical significance - In Mania, there are four stages of mood elevation – euphoria, elation, exultation and ecstasy. Similarly in Depression – degree of low mood can be mild, moderate or severe. Determining the intensity of mood is vital for diagnosis and developing plan for treatment.

3. Duration

Question – How long you have been feeling this way?

Document – Duration reported by patient in number of weeks.

Clinical significance – It takes at least two weeks of low mood to diagnose Depression and one week of mood elevation to diagnose Mania. The duration is a mandatory criterion for the diagnosis.

4. Stability

Question - Does your mood keeps changing?

Document – Stable/ Labile.

Clinical significance - Labile mood can be suggestive of Organic Disorders, Schizophrenia, Personality Disorders or Mood Disorders.

5. Appropriateness

Mood is supposed to react to stimuli. It must have a synchronized relationship with thought.

Example – A person who talks about grandiose ideas is expected to report elevated mood. Similarly an individual with overwhelming guilt is supposed to disclose low mood.

Clinical significance - Inappropriate mood to thought can suggest Schizophrenia.

B. Affect

Affect is the outward, objective expression of immediate, cross-sectional experience of emotion. It is how the interviewer describes a patient's visible expressions. If mood is the symptom, then affect can be compared to sign.

In MSE, Affect is assessed under following heads -

1. Quality

Document – Euthymic/ cheerful/ sad/ irritated/ angry/ agitated/ anxious/ bright/ elated/ euphoric.

Clinical significance – Elated affect is suggestive of Mania. Sad in Depression, fearful in Phobia, Angry in Schizophrenia, Anxious in Anxiety Disorders, Irritable in Hypomania are other common findings.

2. Range

Change of expressions can be noted during the interview by deliberately changing the topic from happy to sad or anger-provoking.

Document – Full/ broad/ labile/ shallow/ restricted/ blunted/ flat.

Clinical significance – Full, broad, exaggerated affect suggests Mania, lability or rapid shifting of expressions indicates Organic Disorders. Whereas, shallow, restricted, blunted (diminished and constricted to a narrow neutral range) and flat (no affective response at all) are suggestive of Schizophrenia.

3. Congruence

Affect is incongruent when it is contradicting with the mood.

Example - Laughing while reporting a low mood or talking about being happy with a gloomy face.

Document – Congruant/ Incongruant.

Clinical significance – Incongruence may suggest Pseudobulbar palsy or Frontal lobe lesions.

Points to ponder

- Mood is subjective and assessed under the heads of quality, intensity, duration, stability and appropriateness
- Affect is objective and assessed under the heads of quality, range and congruence.

CHAPTER 5

Perception

There is no truth, only perception of truth. – Dr Phil

In an over-simplified manner, humans have five senses: vision (optic), hearing (audition), smell (olfaction), taste (gustation), and touch (tactile). In addition to this, there are sensory systems that provide information about balance (vestibular sense), body position and movement (proprioception and kinesthesia), pain (nociception) and temperature (thermoception). A stimulus reaches a physiological threshold (absolute threshold) when it is strong enough to excite sensory receptors and send nerve impulses to the brain. This detection of stimulus by receptors is known as sensation. A message below the absolute threshold is called subliminal - received, but does not generate conscious awareness.

Perception is meaningful organization, interpretation, and conscious experience of sensation. It involves both bottom-up processing (perception is built from sensory inputs) and top-down processing (the interpretation of sensation is influenced by available knowledge, past experiences and thought).

Sensation is a physiological process, whereas perception is psychological. For example - upon walking into a kitchen and smelling the scent of asafoetida, the sensation is the scent receptors detecting, but the perception may be "It smells like the lentils mother used to make in sunday afternoons."

The factors which may interfere with perception in normal scenario are -

Sensory adaptation - Stimuli that remain relatively constant over prolonged periods of time, are generally not perceived. For example – odour in a damp room one gets used to after some time, whereas a person who enters the room, gets the smell instantly.

Inattentional blindness - Failure to notice something that is completely visible because of lack of attention.

Motivation – As per Signal Detection theory, motivation can enhance human ability to discriminate between a true sensory stimulus and background noise. For example - A mother is awakened by a quiet murmur from her baby but not by other sounds that occur while she is asleep.

Perceptual disorders can be broadly classified under following heads -

A. Sensory Distortion

1. Intensity

Question – Do you perceive any change in the intensity of any sensory stimuli?

Document – Change in tactile sensation (Hyperesthesia or Hypoesthesia), Hearing (Hyperacousis or Hypoacousis), Pain sensation (Hyperalgesia or Hypoalgesia)

Clinical significance – Hyperesthesia is suggestive of exaggerated emotion, acute Psychoses, intoxication with psychedelic substance and Epileptic aura. On the other hand Hypoesthesia denotes Depression and Delirium. Hyperacousis can manifest in Hypochondriacal personalities and Anxiety Disorders, whereas Hypoacousis is present in Delirium.

2. Quality

Question - Do you perceive any change in the appearance of any sensory stimuli?

Document – Presence of Xanthopsia (yellow vision), Chloropsia (green vision), Erythropsia (red vision), change in taste or smell.

Clinical significance – Changes in quality of stimuli suggest organic disorders and substance use.

3. Space

Question – Can you perceive the right size or distance of any sensory stimuli?

Document – Presence of Macropsia (things appear larger or nearer than they actually are), Micropsia (things appear smaller or farther than they actually are).

Clinical significance – Dysmegalopsia (changes in spatial form) suggests ophthalmic concerns, temporal lobe lesions, Schizophrenia and Delirium.

4. Time

When we are happy time flies, but when we are sad it drags.

Clinical significance – In severe Depression, passage of time is perceived very slow and it may even appear standstill. Whereas in Mania it may appear faster than normal. In acute Schizophrenia, patient perceives the time seems to go by fits and starts. Temporal lobe lesion, hyperthermia, post-encephalitic states and oculogyric crisis are some common organic conditions where disturbance in time estimation takes place.

B. Sensory Deception

i) Illusion – It is defined as misinterpretation of sensory stimuli. In illusion, a stimulus is combined with a mental image which produces a false perception.

Example – A shadow of a shrub might appear like a man with a baggage.

Clinical significance - In majority of the cases, illusions do not have any psychopathology. But frequent illusions are suggestive of organic disorders.

ii) Hallucination – It is a perception experienced in the absence of any external stimuli.

Classification of Hallucinations on the basis of sensory domain involved

a. Auditory hallucinations

Q 1 - Have you ever heard things that other people could not hear?

Q 2 - Have you ever heard things that later turned out not to be there?

Q 3 - Is it sounds (elementary) or voices (complex)?

Q 4 - Do you recognize the voice or the gender?

Q 5 - What is the content?

Q 6 - Is it a command to harm yourself or others?

Document – Auditory hallucination/ command hallucination with verbatim

Clinical significance – Auditory hallucination is the commonest form in non-organic psychosis.

b. Visual hallucinations

Q 1 - Have you ever seen things that other people could not see?

Q 2 - Have you ever seen things that later turned out not to be there

Q 3 - Describe what you saw.

Document – Elementary visual hallucination (flash of light), partly organized (patterns) or completely organized (people, animals or objects)

Clinical significance – Visual hallucination is common in acute organic conditions with clouding of consciousness. Small animals like rats, mice or spiders are most commonly hallucinated in Delirium. Micropsia might lead to Lilliputian hallucination in which tiny people are visualized.

c. Olfactory hallucination

Clinical significance - This can be found in patients with Schizophrenia, organic disorders, temporal lobe epilepsy and less commonly, in Depression.

d. Tactile hallucination – Commonest form is formication (animals are crawling over the body). Other forms are sensation of cold winds, heat, electric impulse and sexual.

Clinical significance – Formication is seen in acute organic states and cocaine bugs. Other variants can be seen in Schizophrenia.

e. Gustatory hallucination

Clinical significance - Can be present in organic cases and Schizophrenia.

Special type of hallucinations

a. Hypnagogic and Hypnopompic hallucinations - Hallucinations that occur while falling asleep (hypnagogic) and while waking up from sleep (hypnopompic).

Example – Hearing his own name being called.

Clinical significance – Usually non-pathological and may be considered within the realm of normal experience.

b. Functional hallucination – Hallucination is accompanied by a provoking stimulus to the same sensory domain and both are experienced at the same time.

Example – Hearing voices with the birds chirping.

Clinical significance - This is experienced in patients with Schizophrenia.

c. Synesthesia/ Reflex hallucination – Stimulation in one sensory field produces hallucination to another.

Example – A patient might feel a pain triggered when another patient sneezed.

Clinical significance - This can be associated with intoxication with psychedelic substance.

d. Extracampine hallucination – Hallucination experienced outside physiological limits of sensory domains.

Example – Hearing a voice from miles away or being able to see behind one's own head.

Clinical significance - This can suggest organic disorder, Schizophrenia or hypnagogic hallucinations.

e. Scenic/Panoramic hallucination – Vivid, continuous, complex hallucination like a movie.

Example – A alcohol withdrawal patient in delirium had an experience where he hallucinated a group of cavalries came to attack him and he could simultaneously hear the hooves galloping.

Clinical significance - Common in patients with temporal lobe epilepsy.

f. Autoscopy/ Doppelganger – In this strange experience, the individual sees one's own self. It is not a simple visual hallucination, it involves kinaesthetic and somatic sensation which gives an impression to the subject that the image is himself. Internal autoscopy is a condition reported by French psychiatrists where subjects see their own internal organs. Negative autoscopy, on the other hand is a condition where the individual is not able to see his own image in the mirror.

Clinical significance – Autoscopy can be seen in normal subjects when they are emotionally very disturbed or physically exhausted associated with altered state of consciousness. It is often associated with disorders of parietal lobe due to cerebrovascular pathology or severe CNS infection. Drug addiction and chronic alcoholism may also be a precursor of autoscopy.

g. Pseudohallucination – Clear and vivid mental images lacks substantiality of a perception.

Clinical significance - Possibly seen in patients with Schizophrenia.

C. Disturbance of Reality Perception

The 'as if' phenomenon.

i) Depersonalization - The person feels detached and views self as strange and unreal.

ii) Derealization - A similar alteration occurs in the reality perception related to outside world.

Clinical significance - May be seen in Depression, Anxiety disorders, organic states and substance use.

iii) Disturbance related to body image - In patients with organic disorders and intoxication with psychedelic substance, perceptual disorders like right-Left disorientation, Anasagnosia (not being aware of the presence of an illness like paralysis), Autopagnosia (inability to recognize one's own body parts), Phantom limb sensation, change in size, shape or location of body part, sensation of floating in space are common.

iv) Somatic passivity - Strange bodily sensation as being imposed by 'some external agency' with the patient being a passive recipient. It is one of the Schneider's first rank symptoms of Schizophrenia

Points to ponder

- Perceptual disorders are classified under three heads – sensory distortion, sensory deception and disorders of reality perception.
- Sensory distortions are assessed under four heads – intensity of stimuli, quality of stimuli, space perception and time perception.
- Sensory deceptions are of two types – illusion and hallucination.
- Hallucination can be classified as per the involvement of sensory domain into five types – visual, auditory, olfactory, tactile and gustatory.
- There are some special types of hallucination – hypnagogic and hypnopompic, synesthesia, extracampine, functional, scenic, autoscopy and pseudo-hallucination.

- Disorders of reality perception can be categorized into – depersonalization, derealization, somatic passivity and disturbance of body image.

CHAPTER 6

Cognitive Functions

Disconnected facts in the mind are like unlinked pages on the Web: They might as well not exist.
- Steven Pinker

Cognitive functions refer to multiple mental activities. The most common areas of cognition evaluated on a MSE are consciousness, orientation, attention, concentration, memory, judgment, general intelligence, fund of information, abstract thinking and level of insight.

A. Consciousness

Consciousness can be defined as a state of awareness of self and environment with a degree of reactivity.

1. Level of consciousness

Consciousness ranges from alertness to coma with intervening stages. It may also be referred as quantitative alteration of consciousness.

i) Alertness - Patient is fully awake and can respond to stimuli.

ii) Clouding of consciousness – Features confusion and disorientation.

Clinical significance – Marks Delirium.

iii) Somnolence - A reduced level of consciousness where the patient is lethargic or drowsy, but able to perceive stimuli and can be awakened fairly easily.

Clinical significance – Suggests substance intoxication.

iv) Obtundation – Strong stimuli needed to arouse the patient, and when awoken patient will be drowsy with delayed response.

Clinical significance – Indicates head injury, hypoxia, hypercapnia, central nervous system infections, drug intoxication or withdrawal, post-seizure state, hypothermia, and metabolic derangements such as hypoglycemia, hyponatremia and hypercalcaemic crisis.

v) Stupor - Unresponsive to all except painful stimuli.

vi) Coma - Unresponsive to all stimuli, including vigorous and noxious stimuli.

Clinical significance – Suggests a metabolic cause like hypoglycemia.

2. Restriction of consciousness

Awareness sometimes is narrowed down to fewer ideas and attitudes which dominates the patient's mind. This can be considered qualitative changes of consciousness.

i) Twilight state – The term was introduced by Westphal to describe a condition in which there is a break in the continuity of consciousness in the presence of relatively well-ordered behavior.

Clinical significance – Most common in post-Epilepsy.

ii) Fugue – Physical and psychological flight (wandering) from one's usual place with some amnesia. To some patients, amnesia sounds like a temporary solution to their anxiety producing problems. So they 'forget' their identity and past life.

Clinical significance – May follow history of head injury with concussion.

B. Orientation

Orientation is patient's awareness of their situation and surroundings normally described in terms of time, place and person. When consciousness is disturbed, it affects these three aspects in that order.

Q 1 - Time, Date, Day, Month, Season, Year, Duration of hospitalization.

Q 2 – Place, Building, City, Country.

Q 3 – Person, identification of self and others.

Clinical significance - Most common in organic states, rarely seen in chronic hospitalized Schizophrenics.

C. Memory

The ability, process or act of remembering or recalling and the ability to reproduce the learning or experience is called memory.

1. Immediate Retention and Recall

The ability to register information is called immediate memory.

Step 1 (Retention) - Dictate five unrelated objects or concepts (like – fish, pencil, violet, anger and fire), or a short sentence, or a five-component name and address. Instruct the subject to pay attention because he has to repeat them immediately, first forward and then backward.

Step 2 (Recall) - After five minutes of performing a second, unrelated mental task, ask the patient to repeat the words.

Inference – If the subject is able to recall at least four out of five words, immediate memory is considered intact. If two to four words recalled, it is subjected to further evaluation. Less than two suggests impairment.

Clinical significance - Cortical lesions of the dominant hemisphere tend to result in impairment of verbal retention, while non-dominant hemispheric lesions with projections to the hippocampi result in nonverbal retention deficits.

2. Recent Memory

The ability to remember the events of last few days is called recent memory.

Question – What did you have for breakfast last morning?

Clinical significance - Impaired memory may point to a neurocognitive disorder, an amnestic syndrome like Korsakoffs psychosis, bilateral hippocampal infarction and Herpes Simplex Encephalitis.

3. Remote memory

The ability to recall long-past events is known as long term memory.

Question – What was the name of your primary school?

Clinical significance - Alzheimer's, Parkinson's and Pick's Disease has early symptom of defective short-term memory followed by loss of remote memory.

The disorders of memory

i) Amnesia – Partial or total loss of memory, can be psychogenic or organic.

ii) Confabulation – A false piece of memory which patient believes to be true.

iii) Ganser syndrome – Syndrome of approximate answers.

Example – If the examiner asks 'How many legs does the cat have?', patient might answer 'Three' or 'Five' but not 'Four'.

iv) Déjà vu – Feeling of familiarity with unfamiliar things, which has the following variance -

- **Deja pense** – Feeling that he has already thought of the matter.
- **Deja enterndu** – Feeling that one has heard before what he is hearing now.
- **Deja raconte** – A forgotten experience from distant past is recalled and individual feels the incident is told to him by someone else.
- **Deja eprouve** – The feeling that an act has already been carried out by a patient, in which he was never actually engaged.
- **Deja fait** – A feeling that what is happening to the patient now, has happened before.

V) Jamais vu – A phenomenon operationalized as the opposite of déjà vu, characterized by unfamiliarity in situation which is not novel.

D. Attention and Concentration

1. Attention

It is conscious and willful focusing of mental energy on one object or one component of a complex experience.

Test - Digit Span Test – Forward and backward counting

- Forward and backward spelling

2. Concentration

It is sustained attention to the same stimuli.

Test – Counting months forward and backward

- Serial 7 Subtraction Test (100-7 and so on)
- Serial 3 Subtraction Test (50-3 and so on)

Clinical significance - Impairment in attention/concentration may be seen in fatigue, Anxiety, Depression, Schizophrenia, substance use or neurocognitive disorders.

E. Abstraction

Abstract thinking is the ability of voluntary assumption of a mental set, shift from one aspect to another aspect of a situation, simultaneous consideration of various aspects, synthesis and analysis of a content.

Test – Similarities and dissimilarities between objects, like laptop and cellphone.

- Explanation of a proverb, like 'All that glitters is not gold'.

Clinical significance - Literal interpretations and answers indicate concrete thinking, which is seen in Psychoses, some intellectual disabilities and neurocognitive disorders.

F. Judgment

This refers to the ability to draw direct conclusions from the material acquired by experience.

1. Test Judgment

Patient's prediction what he would do in a hypothetical situation.

Question – What would you do if this room catches fire?

2. Social Judgment

Patient's attitude toward a particular social phenomenon.

Question – Do you think violence against women is justified?

3. Personal Judgment

Patient's attitude towards self.

Question – What will you do when you are discharged from the hospital?

Clinical significance - Impaired judgment suggests Psychoses and organic disorders.

G. General intelligence and fund of information

This part of cognitive function is assessed by administering simple arithmetic and general knowledge questions.

Clinical significance – A deficit in this area may suggest Dementia or Schizophrenia.

H. Insight

It refers to the subjective awareness of the pathological nature of psychiatric symptoms and behavioral disturbances.

There are six different levels of insight which can be assessed with a single question-

Question – Do you think you have a mental disorder?

i. Complete denial – Absent insight.

Response – 'No, never. I am perfectly alright.'

ii. Slight awareness – Awareness of being sick but denies help.

Response – 'Something different but definitely not mental disorder.'

iii. Awareness of external factor– Aware but attributes it to some external or physiological factor like exhaustion, sleep deprivation, irregular eating habit or black magic.

Response – 'I had a crying spell because my boss assigned excessive amount of work, I do not get to sleep enough or have time to eat'.

iv. Awareness of unknown – Aware but attributes it to something unknown as the patient started doubting the presence of any external or physiological factor.

Response – 'I don't understand what's happening to me, I feel like crying all the time, don't get enough sleep either'.

v. Intellectual insight - Admits having mental disorder based on rational interpretation of experience.

Response - 'Since this medicine has improved my sleep pattern and the doctor also says, I may be having some irrational beliefs which are not normal.'

vi. Emotional insight – Accepts from within the presence of mental illness.

Response – 'Yes, I have mental disorder and I need treatment for the same'.

Clinical significance – Impaired or absent insight is suggestive of Psychoses.

Points to ponder

- Cognitive functions are assessed under nine headings – consciousness, orientation, memory, attention, concentration, abstract thinking, judgment, intelligence and general information and insight to the illness.
- Disorders of consciousness are divided into lowering of consciousness and restriction of consciousness.
- Lowering of consciousness can be ranging anywhere between alertness, clouding, somnolence, obtundation, stupor and coma.
- Restricted consciousness can be twilight state or fugue.
- Orientation is assessed in respect of time, place and person.
- Memory is assessed under immediate, recent and remote categories.
- Disorders of memory are amnesia, confabulation, Ganser syndrome, deja vu and jamais vu.
- Attention, concentration, abstract thinking and intelligence have specific tests.
- Judgment is assessed under three heads – situational, personal and social.
- There are six levels of insight – complete denial, slight awareness, awareness of external factor, awareness of unknown origin, intellectual and true emotional insight.

CHAPTER 7

Application

Sitting on your shoulders is the most complicated object in the known universe. - Michio Kaku

By the virtue of technological explosion, the molecular configuration of the basic structural unit of human body like the nephron, islet cell or myofibril is well visualized. However the brain continues to be the "black box" and can only be attempted to observe, test and codify the mystery through behaviour.

A. Bio-drives

Physiological needs like hunger, sleep or sex are the biological beginnings that eventually manifest themselves as a psychological drive in a person's subjective awareness, known as bio-drives.

Mental disorders are largely manifested as altered bio-drives. Hence, after assessing the previously stated components of MSE, it is important to explore the bio-drives.

1. Sleep

Changes may occur in pattern, quality and duration of sleep in psychological distress.

Clinical significance – Manic usually has decreased need for sleep, insomnia is present in Depression and Anxiety. Depressive may also complaint of nonrefreshing sleep. Reverse sleep-wake pattern and hypersomnia can be is seen in Delirium.

2. Appetite

Clinical significance – Appetite significantly changes in Psychoses, mood disorders and Anxiety. Person may forget to eat in Dementia, Manic may not find time to eat because of hyperactivity.

3. Libido

Clinical significance – A decrease in libido is seen in Depression, Anxiety and certain drug use, whereas an increase is seen in Mania and certain organic disorders.

4. Activity

Patient may complain of Anergia (lack of energy for activities of daily living) or Anhedonia (inability to experience pleasure in previously pleasurable activities).

Clinical significance – Lack of energy signifies Depression whereas sense of increased energy suggests Mania. Disturbance in volition (the will to act) is seen in Schizophrenia.

B. Provisional diagnosis

MSE can suggest the presence of a particular mental disorder but for a confirmed diagnosis it needs to be supported by a detailed psychiatric history collection, physical examination, psychological tests and investigation report such as neuroimaging, toxicology screening, thyroid function, blood counts and metabolic parameters.

C. Differential diagnosis

Majority of the symptoms in Psychiatry are complex and may be confusing, hence provisional diagnosis can be challenged by differential diagnosis. Hence the diagnosis needs to be established on the bases of the criteria of International Classification of Diseases (ICD) or Diagnostic and Statistical Manual of Mental Disorders (DSM).

Limitations of MSE

- MSE is a subjective assessment of a patient and may vary significantly between examiners based on their knowledge, skill and attitude.
- MSE may not be of much use in case patient has an intellectual disability or neurological disorder.
- Language is an integral part of MSE, hence difference in language between patient and examiner can be a barrier.
- Physiological condition of the patient like mal-nutrition, sleep deprivation, intoxication may interfere with the process.

Conclusion

MSE is not only useful in diagnosing and monitoring a mental disorder, it aids in clinical decision making like course of treatment and need for hospitalization. The mystery of the blackbox can be approximated to a large distance through this process till there is a quantum leap in neuroimaging.

APPENDIX

Format for Mental Status Examination

- Time, Date & Place of Examination –

1. **Patient's particulars**

- Name & Age
- Gender
- Ethnicity & Language
- Religion
- Education
- Occupation & Income
- Marital status & No. of children

2. **Appearance & Behaviour**

- Body built - Asthenic/ Athletic/ Pyknic/ Dysplastic
- Age appropriateness - Age appropriate/ Looks older/ Looks younger
- Grooming - Immaculate/ Kempt/ Unkempt
- Clothing – Appropriate/ Inappropriate to weather & occasion
- Gestures - Cooperative/ Relaxed/ Agitated/ Avoidant/ Indifferent/ Guarded/ Evasive/ Hostile/ Combative/ Haughty/ Playful/ Over-friendly/ Hallucinatory/ Compulsive

- Facial expression - Smiling/ Grimacing/ Perplexed/ Apathetic/ Frowning/ Tearful/ Silly smile/ Omega sign/ Veraguth folds
- Eye contact - Direct/ Furtive/ Nil/ Continuous/ Intermittent
- Social etiquettes – Appropriate/ Inappropriate
- Rapport – Built with ease/ Built with difficulty/ Not built at all
- Gait - Dragging of one leg/ Sudden knee buckling or collapse/ Small and slow steps/ Excessive swaying/ Extra movements of arms & legs that disrupt balance/ Crouching/ Anxiety about falling
- Posture - Negativism/ Automatic obedience / Waxy flexibility/ Catalepsy/ Mitmachen/ Cogwheel rigidity
- Movement – Hyperactivity/ Excitement/ Impulsivity/ Akathisia/ Agitation/ Psychomotor Retardation/ Bradykinesia/ Akinesia/ Tics / Mannerisms/ Stereotype/ Perseveration/ Echopraxia

3. Thought & Speech

Thought

- Form – Derailment/ Substitution/ Omission/ Fusion/ Drivelling/ Desultory thinking/ Associative loosening
- Progression - Flight of ideas/ Prolixity/ Retardation/ Blocking/ Perseveration/ Circumstantiality/ Tangentiality
- Content - Overvalued ideas/ Fantasies/ Obsessions/ Phobias/ Ideas of reference/ Delusion

- Control/Possession - Thought alienation

Speech

- Quantity – Normal/ Mutism/ Poverty of speech/ Pressure of speech
- Spontaneity and Reaction time - Normal/ Delayed/ Premature
- Rhythm and Flow – Normal/ Stammering/ Stuttering/ Cluttering/ Slurring/ Dysarthria
- Volume – Normal/ Loud/ Low
- Tone – Appropriate/ Inappropriate
- Language and Vocabulary - Appropriate/ Inappropriate
- Deviations – Neologism/ Echolalia/ Cataphasia/ Verbigeration/ Coprolalia

4. Mood & Affect

Mood

- Quality – 'okay'/ 'happy'/ 'sad'/ 'worried'/ 'irritable'/ 'angry'/ 'detached'/ 'indifferent'
- Intensity - 'Mild'/ 'very'/ 'extremely'
- Duration – In weeks
- Stability – Stable/ Labile
- Appropriateness – Appropriate/ Inappropriate

Affect

- Quality - Euthymic/ cheerful/ sad/ irritated/ angry/ agitated/ anxious/ bright/ elated/ euphoric
- Range - Full/ broad/ labile/ shallow/ restricted/ blunted/ flat

- Congruence - Congruant/ Incongruant

5. Perception

- Change in tactile sensation/ Hearing/ Pain sensation
- Presence of Xanthopsia/ Chloropsia/ Erythropsia/ change in taste or smell
- Presence of Macropsia/ Micropsia
- Time perception- Normal/ Slow/ Fast
- Presence of Illusion/ Hallucination

6. Cognitive Functions

Consciousness

- Level of consciousness – Alertness/ Clouding of consciousness/ Somnolence/ Obtundation/ Stupor/ Coma
- Restriction of consciousness - Twilight state/ Fugue

Orientation

- Oriented to - Time, Date, Day, Month, Season, Year, Duration of hospitalization
- Oriented to – Place, Building, City, Country
- Oriented to – Person – identification of self & others

Memory

- Immediate Retention & Recall of 5 unrelated words – Intact/ Impaired
- Recent Memory last 24 hours - Intact/ Impaired

- Remote memory of personal & impersonal events - Intact/ Impaired
- Presence of Amnesia/ Confabulation/ Ganser syndrome/ Déjà vu/ Jamais vu

Attention

- Attention – Easily arousable/ Aroused with efforts
- Digit Span Test – Able to perform upto which level
- Forward & backward spelling - Able to perform upto which level

Concentration

- Sustained/ Distracted
- Counting forward & backward - Able to perform upto which level
- Serial 7 Subtraction Test (100-7 & so on) - Able to perform upto which level

Abstraction

- Similarities & dissimilarities – Intact/ Impaired
- Explanation of a proverb - Intact/ Impaired

Judgment

- Test – Intact/ Impaired
- Social - Intact/ Impaired
- Personal - Intact/ Impaired

General intelligence & fund of information

- Adequate/Inadequate

7. Insight

- Level 1 - Complete denial
- Level 2 - Slight awareness
- Level 3 - Awareness of external factor
- Level 4 - Awareness of unknown
- Level 5 - Intellectual insight
- Level 6 – True Emotional insight

8. Bio-drives

- Sleep- Unchanged/ Increased/ Decreased; Presence of Somnambulism/ Bruxism/ Nightmare
- Appetite - Unchanged/ Increased/ Decreased; Presence of Pica
- Libido - Unchanged/ Increased/ Decreased; Presence of Paraphilia
- Energy for activity - Unchanged/ Increased/ Decreased

9. Provisional diagnosis

10. Differential diagnosis

Suggested Further Reading

1. Hamilton M. Fish's Clinical Psychopathology – Signs and Symptoms in Psychiatry. Mumbai : Varghese Publishing House; 1985.
2. Bhatia MS. Essentials of Psychiatry. New Delhi: CBS Publishers; 2019.
3. Ahuja N. A Short Textbook of Psychiatry. New Delhi: JayPee Brothers Medical Publishers; 2011.
4. Hoch PM, Zubin J. Psychopathology of Perception. New York: Grune and Stratton Publishers; 1965.
5. Chapman LJ, Chapman JP. A theory of verbal behaviour in Schizophrenia. New York: Academic Press; 1964.
6. Bleuler E. Textbook of Psychiatry. New York: Dover Publication; 1951.
7. Arnold MB. Emotion and Personality. London: Cassell Publication; 1961.
8. King HE. Psychomotor Aspects of Mental Disease. Cambridge: Harvard University Press; 1954.
9. American Psychiatric Association. Desk reference to the diagnostic criteria from DSM-5. Arlington: American Psychiatric Association; 2016.
10. The ICD-11 classification of mental and behavioural disorders: Diagnostic criteria for research. Geneva: World Health Organization; 2019/2021. https://icd.who.int/browse11